Contents

Words in **bold** can be found in the glossary on pages 28–29.

Different types of plants

Plants grow in parks, gardens and window boxes in towns and cities, and can even be found in gaps in the pavement or cracks in walls. In the countryside, plants grow everywhere.

Mosses, ferns and conifers

There are four major groups of plants: **mosses**, **ferns**, **conifers** and **flowering plants**.

Mosses grow on stones, tree trunks or close to the soil in damp places with little light. They have small leaves that grow into the shape of little mats or cushions.

Conifers have dark green leaves like needles. They often grow in cold places. Conifers grow **cones** that contain **seeds**.

Ferns have big leaves called **fronds** that look like giant feathers. They usually grow in damp **habitats** with little light.

Flowering plants

This book is about flowering plants. Flowers make and spread **pollen** to make seeds. New plants grow from these seeds. There are two main ways that flowering plants spread pollen. They let the pollen blow away on the wind or they attract insects and other animals, such as birds, with coloured **petals** and scent. The pollen sticks to the insect or animal's body and it is carried away with them.

In this book, flowers that attract insects are called **insect-pollinated** flowers. Flowers that use the wind to carry their pollen are called **wind-pollinated** flowers. They are small green flowers without petals or scent.

Grasses are plants with wind-pollinated flowers. Daisies are plants with insect-pollinated flowers.

Make a list of all the different types of plant you can find in your garden or local park. Decide whether the flowering plants have insect- or wind-pollinated flowers.

Growing roots

A seed is a **capsule** that contains a tiny plant and a supply of food. The first part of the plant to grow out of a seed is the **root**. It grows down into the soil and holds the plant in the ground.

Parts of a root

There is a cap at the end of a root. It makes a kind of slime so the root can move easily through the soil as it grows. Behind the cap, the root grows many long, thin **root hairs**. These grow into the soil and collect water from it. Inside the root are tiny pipes that carry this water up to the plant's **stem**.

Tiny root hairs can be clearly seen on the roots of these cress plants.

Fibrous roots

There are two kinds of roots: **fibrous roots** and **tap roots**. Fibrous roots grow out from the bottom of a plant's stem. They are made up of many small roots of a similar length and thickness. The roots form a mat which grows just below the surface of the soil.

Grass plants have fibrous roots.

Tap roots

A tap root is a long, thick root which grows down deep into the soil. It may have many thick side roots, like a bean plant, or it may have thin roots growing out from it, like a carrot plant.

This bean plant has many side roots growing out of its tap root.

Plant some bean seeds in soil, in clear plastic pots. Make sure the seeds are close to the edge of each pot. Plant each bean seed with a different side pointing upwards, so they are in lots of different positions in the soil. Water the seeds regularly. After a week check the roots. Carefully dig them up if necessary. Do the roots always grow down?

Stems

The stem is the part of a plant that holds up the leaves and flowers. It contains tubes or pipes that are connected to the pipes in the root. Water passes up these pipes to the plant's leaves and flowers. Food made in the leaves (see page 11) passes down a different set of pipes in the stem to all parts of the plant so they can receive energy to stay alive.

Non-woody stems

There are two kinds of stem: the **woody stems** of trees and **shrubs**, and the non-woody stems of **herbaceous** plants, such as the sunflower. Non-woody stems cannot survive in cold weather conditions and so they die back to ground level during the winter, ready to grow again in the spring. They also need plenty of water to hold them up. If the weather is dry, non-woody stems and their leaves **wilt**.

The stems of these herbaceous plants will die back in the winter.

The woody stems of these trees are covered in **bark**, which protects them from the cold weather.

Grow two pots of cress seeds. Keep one pot in a light place and put one in a box. Don't close the box completely. After a week compare their stems. What do you find?

When a woody stem is cut in half, you can see ring shapes. Each ring represents one year of growth.

Woody stems

Woody stems can survive in all weather conditions. They have a layer of bark that prevents them from freezing in cold weather. Inside the stem the water-carrying pipes are arranged in rings.

Leaves

Buds grow on stems. They can contain leaves, tiny shoots and flowers. A plant needs warmth and water to open its buds. When they open, the plant's leaves, shoots and flowers uncurl out of them.

When a bud opens, the leaf stalk grows and pushes out from the stem.

leaf blade

mid-rib

vein

leaf stalk

Mid-rib and veins

In many leaves, there is a thick line that runs down the centre of the **leaf blade**. It is called the **mid-rib** and it has side ribs growing out from it. These side ribs are called **veins**. They support the thin leaf blade and hold it out into the air and the sunlight.

The main features of a leaf.

stem

bud

Leaf shapes

Each plant grows a certain kind of leaf. It might be long and thin, or oval, or divided into points. The leaf edge is called the **margin**. Some leaves have smooth margins, some have wavy margins and some have lots of little points on them. The surface of the blade can also vary. It may be smooth and soft, shiny, waxy or covered in hairs.

Each plant grows leaves of a certain shape and size to help it survive in its habitat.

Compare the shape and margins of leaves from different plants. Can you arrange them into groups, according to their shape? You could group them again according to their margins, such as smooth, pointy or wavy.

Making food

The leaves are the food-making part of the plant. They use water from the roots and a **gas** from the air called carbon dioxide to make food. They also use energy from sunlight. This food-making process in plants is called **photosynthesis**. Some energy from sunlight is stored in the food. The plant uses this energy to grow and stay alive.

Water on the move

Water enters a plant's root through the root hairs. It passes into tiny pipes in the root and moves upwards into the stem. From the stem, the water moves into the leaf stalk, then spreads out into the rest of the leaf.

Transpiration

Inside a leaf blade some water is used to make food, but most of it **evaporates** to form **water vapour**. This escapes from the leaf through the **microscopic** holes in its upper and lower surface in a process called **transpiration**. Warmth in the habitat speeds up transpiration.

Transpiration makes water move through a plant. Water from the leaf veins spreads out into the blade to take the place of the water that has evaporated from the leaf's surface.

Water in the ribs, leaf stalk, stem and root move up to take the place of water in the veins of the leaf blade.

Transpiration test

You can see the path water takes through a celery stalk and its leaves by trying the following experiment.

1.
Find a leafy celery stalk and ask an adult to cut off about a centimetre from the bottom end. Place the cut end in the coloured water and leave it in a warm place.

2.
After a few hours, check to see if the coloured water has entered the pipes in the stalk and in the leaves.

If one celery stalk with its leaves and one without its leaves were dipped in coloured water, which stalk would suck up the coloured water faster? Explain your answer.

Types of flower

At a certain time of year, such as spring or summer, warmth in its habitat makes a flowering plant burst its buds to reveal flowers. Insect-pollinated flowers unfurl their large, colourful petals and release their scent into the air. Wind-pollinated flowers open and release huge quantities of pollen into the air.

Onion flowers are arranged in an umbel (see below). They are pollinated by flying insects.

Umbel and spike flowers

The flowers on a plant may grow on separate stems or in a group. Some groups of flowers grow out in all directions from the top of a stem. This arrangement of flowers is called an umbel. Other flowers grow closely together up a stem. This arrangement is called a spike. The arrangement of flowers can help different kinds of insects to visit them. For example, the flowers on a spike sit high above other plants so they can be seen easily by passing insects.

Foxglove flowers are arranged in a spike. They are pollinated by bees.

A flower head

Many flowers grow in a group on the top of a stem. These flowers are small and tightly packed together. They are called florets. Around a group of florets, the flowers grow a ring of larger petals, as seen in a sunflower. This arrangement of flowers is called a flower head.

Sunflowers are arranged in a flower head. They are pollinated by flying insects.

florets

Look at the flowers in a park, a garden or in the countryside. Which type of flower arrangement do you mostly find – umbel, spike or flower head?

The parts of a flower

While a flower is forming in its bud, it is protected from the weather by **sepals**. These are like small leaves. They fold over the flower and overlap each other to keep out wind and cold weather.

sepals

When a flower is ready to open, the sepals bend outwards to let the flower come out of the bud.

Petals

The outer part of a flower is formed of petals. They can be brightly coloured and often produce a smell to attract insects. The petals may also have lines on them, which guide insects down into the flower to find **nectar**. This is a sweet liquid made at the base of the petals, which insects feed on.

Reproduction

Pollen is made in the **anther**, which is held up by the **filament**. At the centre of many flowers is a **stigma**, which has a sticky surface for catching the pollen. It is held up by a stalk called a **style**. Pollen on the stigma grows tubes through the style into a swelling called the **ovary**, where seeds are produced (see page 20). The seeds will then go on to make new plants. This process is called **reproduction**.

stigma   anther

filament

style   ovary

Some flowers, such as the buttercup, have a group of ovaries at their centre. Each one has its own stigma and style.

Pollination

The ovary of a flower needs pollen before it can make seeds. Pollen grains are microscopic and are made in the anther. When the grains are fully formed, the anther splits open to let them out.

Types of pollen

The pollen grains made by insect-pollinated flowers have a spiky surface. This helps them stick to the hairs on an insect's body. The pollen grains made by wind-pollinated flowers are very light. This helps them to be blown a long way in the wind to find another flower to reproduce with. Wind-pollinated pollen grains are smooth because they do not need to grip onto an insect's body.

These pollen grains from a chicory flower have been magnified in order to see their spiky surface.

The flowers on a tomato plant can self-pollinate.

Self-pollination

There are two kinds of pollination. The first is called self-pollination. This is where the pollen simply falls from the anther to the stigma of the same flower. Self-pollination helps plants to reproduce in places where there is little wind or few insects, such as in mountainous habitats.

Pollen from one flower sticks to an insect. The insect takes the pollen with it as it moves to a new flower.

Cross-pollination

The second kind of pollination is called cross-pollination. This takes place when the pollen from the anther of one flower lands on the stigma of another flower of the same kind of plant. Cross-pollination helps plants growing close together to reproduce in habitats where there are plenty of insects and wind.

?

How are the two types of pollen different? How are they similar?

Making seeds and fruits

After pollination has taken place, the plant is ready to make seeds from which new plants will grow.

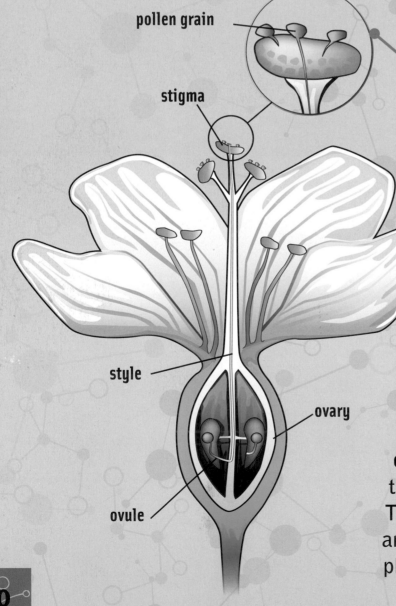

pollen grain

stigma

style

ovary

ovule

A seed is made when the contents of a pollen grain join with the ovule.

Fertilisation

When a pollen grain lands on a stigma, the grain grows a tube. This tube goes down the style and into the ovary. The contents of the pollen grain pass down the tube, too. The end of the tube enters an **ovule**. This is the part of the plant that is ready to become a seed. The pollen contents enter the ovule and join with it. This joining of plant parts is called **fertilisation**.

Spreading seeds

After fertilisation, the ovule grows into a seed and the ovary grows into a **fruit** surrounding the seeds. The purpose of fruits is to help the seeds spread out as far as possible for the best chance of survival. Many fruits use animals to carry the seeds away. Other fruits use the wind to spread out the seeds.

Some fruits, like the burdock, have spikes, which stick to animal fur and feathers.

Some fruits, such as apples and berries, are juicy and good to eat. Animals eat the fruits and move away from the plant. Seeds are then left behind in the animal's droppings.

These dandelion fruits grow parachutes or wings to help the seeds blow away.

21

Air and water

Plants need the carbon dioxide in the air, water and light to survive. They also need **nutrients** from the soil (see page 26).

Gases

Carbon dioxide in the air is taken in by the leaves and used to make food for the plant. Oxygen is produced in the leaves as the plant makes food and this escapes into the air. Water plants take in carbon dioxide that has **dissolved** in water. When oxygen escapes from the plants, it forms bubbles and rises to the water's surface.

The bubbles from this water lily will pop and oxygen will spread out into the air.

Water experiment

Plant roots take up water and use it to make food to help the plant survive. What happens if a plant does not get enough water?

Equipment:

• two identical plants
• watering can

1.
Water two identical plants, such as bean plants, cress plants or pansies, which have been used here.

2.
Place them in a warm, sunny place for a few days. Water one of the plants every day, but do not water the other plant.

Wilting

The plant that is watered stays healthy, but the other one wilts. If the wilting plant is given water it will become healthy again. If the plant is not given any more water, it will eventually die.

? Humans and animals need oxygen to breathe. How do plants help make the air ready for us to breathe?

Plants and light

A seed contains a tiny plant and a store of food. When a seed starts to grow in the soil, the food is used to provide the energy to grow a root to find water and a stem to find light. When a stem grows out of the soil, it grows leaves. The leaves need sunlight to make more food so the plant can keep on growing.

Equipment:

- two identical plants
- watering can
- sunny windowsill
- dark room or bowl to cover plant

Light experiment

What happens to a plant that cannot find light? Try this experiment to find out.

1.
Take two identical plants, such as bean plants, cress plants or pansies, which have been used here. Put one plant in the dark and one in the light.

2.
Look at them every day and make sure they are both watered regularly, so the soil always feels moist. Note how well the stems are growing.

Thin stems and pale leaves

The plant in the dark should grow long, thin stems as it tries to find the light. It should grow smaller, paler leaves too. If it were put back in the dark, the plant would not be able to produce food and would eventually die. The plant kept in the light would continue to grow lots of dark green leaves.

3.
After about ten days, compare the stems of the plants.

Many of the plants in the shade of these trees have died because their leaves have not got enough light to survive.

Light and space

Seeds usually need space around them to grow well. If plants grow too closely together, the leaves of one plant can block light from reaching the leaves of another. In these habitats some plants, such as dandelions, do not survive because they cannot get enough light.

Look at how leaves are arranged on different plant stems. What do you find? Are they placed underneath each other or far apart?

25

Nutrients in the soil

Plants make food in their leaves from light, water and carbon dioxide in the air. They also need some nutrients to help them grow.

Minerals

Plants get nutrients from the soil. These nutrients are called **minerals**. Some of the minerals come from the rocky part of the soil and some come from the **humus**. Humus is the rotten-down remains of dead plants and animals that have fallen to the ground.

Plants can grow in humus made from manure.

How minerals are used

The minerals in soil dissolve in water from rain. As the root grows, the root hairs take in water from the soil and the minerals dissolved in it. As the water passes up the plant through its pipes, the minerals are carried along too. When the minerals reach the leaves, they help the plant make food to keep it growing. When the plant dies, the minerals return to the soil to be used again when new plants start to grow.

The leaves on this potato plant have turned yellow and brown through lack of nutrients.

How do the minerals in a dead leaf become minerals in a new leaf?

27

Glossary

Anther the pollen-making part of a stamen.

Bark the outer covering of a woody plant.

Bud a swelling on a stem in which a leaf or flower grows.

Capsule a small container.

Cones part of a coniferous plant that makes seeds.

Conifer a woody plant with needle-like leaves that makes seeds in cones.

Dissolve a process in which a substance separates and spreads out in a liquid and seems to disappear.

Evaporate a process in which a liquid changes into a gas.

Fern a plant that grows in shady places and has large fronds.

Fertilisation (in plants) a process in which a tiny part of a plant joins with a tiny part of the same type of plant to make a new plant.

Fibrous root a short, thin root which grows together with lots of other roots.

Filament the part of the stamen that holds up the anther.

Flowering plant a plant that grows flowers, which produce fruits and seeds.

Frond the large leaf produced by ferns.

Fruit a part of a flower that forms after fertilisation. It contains the seeds.

Gas a material that has no fixed shape or volume. Gases flow and can be squashed.

Habitat the home of a living thing.

Herbaceous used to describe plants that do not have woody stems. The stems die back in winter time and new ones grow the following year.

Humus a substance in the soil made from animal droppings and the dead bodies of plants and animals.

Insect-pollinated used to describe flowers that use insects to take their pollen between them.

Leaf blade the broad, flat part of a leaf held up by ribs and veins.

Margin the edge of a leaf.

Microscopic objects that are so small that they can only be seen clearly with a microscope.

Mid-rib the thickened part down the middle of a leaf. It is packed with pipes that carry water into the leaf and food away from the leaf.

Minerals chemicals found in soil that plants need for healthy growth.

Moss a small plant that often grows on rocks. It has leaves and stems but no flowers or proper roots.

Nectar a liquid containing sugar that animals drink to give them energy.

Sepals small leaves that grow over a flower and protect it as it forms in a bud.

Shrub a woody plant that is smaller than a tree.

Stem a part of the plant that supports the branches, leaves and flowers and transports water to them from the root.

Stigma the sticky surface in a flower that catches pollen grains.

Style a stalk that holds up the stigma.

Tap root a long, thick root with side roots.

Transpiration the evaporation of water from the surface of a plant.

Veins tiny thickenings that form patterns in the leaf blade. They contain pipes carrying water and food.

Water vapour water in the form of gas.

Wilt the bending of the stem and leaves of a herbaceous plant when it does not receive enough water.

Wind-pollinated used to describe flowers that uses the wind to take the pollen between them.

Woody stem a stem which contains wood to hold it up.

Nutrient a substance that is needed by a living thing to keep it healthy.

Ovary the part of the flower where the ovules and seeds are made.

Ovule the part of the flower that becomes a seed.

Petal part of a flower. Petals are often brightly coloured and may have a scent to attract animals.

Photosynthesis the process in which green plants use light, water and carbon dioxide to make food.

Pollen a yellow dust made of tiny grains that helps plants reproduce.

Reproduction a process in which new plants and animals are made.

Root the part of the plant that holds it in the ground and takes up water and dissolved minerals from the soil.

Root hairs the tiny hairs found on plant roots, which collect water from soil.

Seed a capsule which contains a tiny plant and its store of food.

Answers to the activities and questions

Page 5 Different types of plants

Activity: This will depend on the area you examine. Look for moss on walls, pavements and stones. Look for ferns in shady places. Most plants you find will be flowering plants. Insect-pollinated flowers will be brightly coloured with scent to attract insects.

Page 7 Growing roots

Activity: The roots always grow down.

Page 9 Stems

Activity: The stems in the light will grow straight upwards. The stems in the box will bend and grow towards the light.

Page 11 Leaves

Activity: This will depend on the plants. If there are a number of different plants you may be able to sort the leaves according to the surface of the blade: waxy, shiny, soft, smooth or covered in hairs.

Page 13 Water on the move

Answer: The one with leaves, because leaves provide the place for transpiration to take place. The coloured water moves through the plant to replace the water lost through transpiration.

Page 15 Types of flower

Activity: This will depend on the types of flowers in your area of study. If there are lots of grass plants in your garden or park their flowers will be packed together into spikes.

Page 19 Pollination

Answer: Pollen grains made by insect-pollinated flowers have a spiky surface. Pollen grains made by wind-pollinated flowers have a smooth surface and are very light in weight. They are both microscopic.

Page 23 Air and water

Answer: Plants take in carbon dioxide, which humans and animals breathe out. They release oxygen into the air which replaces the oxygen the humans and animals breathe in.

Page 25 Plants and light

Activity: Leaves are spaced out along the stem. They may be arranged alternately down the stem or arranged in pairs at right-angles to each other. Some may grow out of the stem slightly out of line with the ones above so they can receive light.

Page 27 Nutrients in the soil

Activity: Dead leaves rot and form humus. The minerals in the humus dissolve in water. When water is lost from a plant's leaves in transpiration, the root takes in water containing the minerals. The water passes up the pipes in the root and stem, then into the mid-rib, and veins. The minerals are used in the food-making process in the leaf blade. The minerals in the food are then taken to the flower. When the flower is fertilised the minerals enter the seed. The seed will grow to form a new plant with new leaves.

Index

About this book

Moving Up with Science is designed to help children develop the following skills:

Science enquiry skills: researching using secondary sources, all pages; grouping and classifying, pages 5, 11, 15 and 25; observing over time, pages 7 and 13; comparative and fair testing, pages 7, 9 and 25.

Working scientifically skills: making careful observations, pages 5, 11, 13, 15 and 25; setting up a practical enquiry, pages 7, 9 and 13; making a comparative or fair test, pages 9 and 25; using results to draw simple conclusions, pages 5, 13, 15 and 25; using straightforward scientific evidence to answer questions, pages 7 and 9.

Critical thinking skills: knowledge, all pages; comprehension, page 13; analysis, pages 19, 23 and 27.